Contents

What's Special about Wildflowers?

Naturalists fit all living things into distinct categories: fungi, flowers, insects, mammals and so on. Nature herself has created more of a tangled web. For example wild orchids and many other plants depend for their very existence on the invisible fungal threads that pervade the soil they grow in. Insects need wildflowers, just as the future of most of the flowers is dependent upon pollination by insects. Many of our songbirds feed almost exclusively on flower seeds and berries, as do some small mammals. Every part of this complex web is vital to the others; all are invaluable and irreplaceable.

The most striking evidence of increasing environmental damage over the past half century or so has been an unremitting reduction in the abundance and distribution of so many of what were once very common wild plants and animals. Intensive farming - in particular the removal of hedges, cultivation of formerly permanent pasture, and widespread use of herbicides and pesticides - has created an impoverished ecological landscape capable of supporting very little in the way of wildlife. Foxes are now more often seen in towns than in the countryside; songbirds are more plentiful in suburban gardens than in most farm meadows; and some wildflowers that were once commonplace in the countryside are now rarities surviving only in a few isolated Sites of Special Scientific Interest or, more often, as cultivated varieties in gardens.

We now have clear evidence that Man's activities are changing the climate of our planet and affecting its ecology. Animals can move away from inhospitable areas, and because we don't expect to see the same numbers in the same places every day a serious decline in animal populations can go unnoticed for quite some time. Wildflowers cannot move away from danger, and so they are an immediately obvious barometer of the health of our environment. Several species have already become extinct and many more are endangered. When the flowers disappear they do not go alone; they are telling us that all life, including ours, is at risk.

In recent times the Government's contribution to conservation has been largely focused on rare species and habitats. They are important, of course, but in many instances the main threat to their survival comes not from within those special sites but from the way we treat the surrounding land and, ultimately, the rest of our environment.

Towards a better future for wildflowers

A notable example is the Lady's Slipper Orchid, *Cypripedium calceolus* (right). Victorian plant collectors reduced it to the verge of extinction, and since the 1970s the only known surviving wild plant in Britain has been guarded throughout the flowering period in its Yorkshire site. Now, thanks to a wild plant breeding programme, former locations of this lovely orchid are being recolonised and in some of these the reintroductions have already flowered.

Past generations valued wildflowers much more than society does today, when so few young people can identify even the most common of species. What pleasures they miss by not pausing to wonder at the intricate beauty of a cowslip, a harebell, a violet! Encouraging more people to take an interest in the natural world will be a crucial step towards changing our culture from one of exploitation of natural resources to one of living and working *with* Nature. Fortunately, in Wales there are still many wonderful oases of unspoilt wildflower habitats, alive with the hum of insects and the songs of birds. The challenge to us all is to spread this diversity and abundance more widely by making much more of our countryside, our parks and our gardens hospitable towards wildflowers.

Winter aconite *(Eranthis hyemalis)*

Native to mainland Europe but now naturalised in woods in parts of eastern Wales, this lovely herald of spring, with its golden flowers and light green leaves, often appears well ahead of the first snowdrops.

Winter aconites have underground corms from which emerge the yellow flowers, each with its characteristic ruff-like bracts. The flowers close at night and do not open up by day unless the air temperature rises above 10 degrees Celsius.

A member of the buttercup family, Ranunculaceae, winter aconite is also known as winterling.

Jan Feb Mar Apr May Jun Jul Aug Sep Oct Nov Dec

Snowdrop *(Galanthus nivalis)*

< 20mm >

It is far from clear whether snowdrops are truly native to Wales; most colonies of this member of the lily family almost certainly began as garden escapes, spreading only slowly because these early spring flowers reproduce mainly by division of the bulbs.

Where shaded ground lies undisturbed for many years, snowdrops multiply and form brilliant white and green carpets in early spring, as they have in this ancient churchyard (left) near the Welsh border.

Primrose *(Primula vulgaris)*

>40mm<

Perhaps the best known of all wildflowers, primroses herald the birth of spring. It is as if they prompt the many other wildflowers to follow their example and burst into bloom. These carpeting plants share habitats with wood anemones, violets and lesser celandines.

Occasionally, on woodland edges well away from houses or managed parkland, pink or mauve primroses occur; some of these may well be wildflowers rather than garden escapes.

Jan   Feb   Mar   Apr   May   Jun   Jul   Aug   Sep   Oct   Nov   Dec

Cowslip *(Primula veris)*

> 10mm <

Although they are less common than primroses, cowslips can be found in most parts of Wales. They are easily destroyed by over-cropping of grassland, and so steep roadside verges and the edges of woodland are where they are now most often to be found.

These dainty wildflowers have been given a great many common names, including buckles, palsywort, paigle, peggle, fairy cups, plumrocks, and Our Lady's keys. Although most cowslip flowers are bright yellow, these promiscuous members of the primrose family are not averse to cross breeding and they do occasionally provide displays of orange flowers.

When cowslips and primroses cross pollinate, the result is infertile hybrids known as **false oxlips**. (An example is shown on the left.) There is also a true oxlip species, but its distribution is restricted to just a few localised areas in eastern England and it has never been recorded in Wales.

Jan   Feb   Mar   Apr   May   Jun   Jul   Aug   Sep   Oct   Nov   Dec   *9*

Butterbur *(Petasites hybridus)*

< 140mm >

Commonly known as butterbur, this strange plant begins blooming in spring before many of its leaves appear. The leaves continue growing for several months after the flowers have died and can attain a diameter of a metre by the middle of summer.

< 20mm >

Pictured on the left is a closely related species, *Petasites fragrans,* which has much smaller leaves. Commonly known as **winter heliotrope** (but often also referred to as butterbur) this more common wildflower blooms from December through to March.

Butterbur leaves were used to wrap butter in the days before refrigerators. The leaves are large, pliable, and thick enough to protect the butter and soak up any that melts; they are also pleasantly cool to the touch.

Jan   Feb   Mar   Apr   May   Jun   Jul   Aug   Sep   Oct   Nov   Dec

Lungwort *(Pulmonaria officinalis)*

Also known as soldiers and sailors, this sprawling two-tone wildflower, from which many cultivars have been derived, originated in mainland Europe.

< 10mm >

A spring flower of the borage family (Boraginaceae), lungwort thrives in Wales in damp, shady places such as woodland glades and the base of hedge banks.

The name lungwort probably refers to the white-spotted leaves as suggesting a popular impression of what the insides of diseased lungs might look like.

Lesser Celandine *(Ranunculus ficaria)*

>20mm<

This is one the most abundant and widespread of spring flowers. Although sometimes seen in sunny spots, celandines seem to prefer damp, partially shaded locations. Rarely more than 15cm tall, this member of the buttercup family, Ranunculaceae, brings a welcome splash of early season colour. The glossy flowers usually have eight petals, but occasionally you will find them with as few as seven petals or as many as thirteen.

< 25mm >

When people talk about celandines, it is to the lesser celandine that they are almost invariably referring. Despite its common name, the **greater celandine**, *Chelidonium majus*, is not a close relative but rather a member of the poppy family, and it blooms much later in the year.

Like most other poppies, the greater celandine can cope with very dry sandy soil, and it is quite commonly seen on steep, fast-draining sunny banks throughout Wales.

Jan   Feb   Mar   Apr   May   Jun   Jul   Aug   Sep   Oct   Nov   Dec

Wood Anemone *(Anemone nemorosa)*

15mm

Wood Anemones, also known as windflowers, are among the most profuse and attractive of woodland flowers. In early spring they carpet the forest floor in a glorious blend of mauves and whites.

Wood anemones are most at home among broadleaved trees rather than under mature evergreen conifers where little sunlight reaches the ground. The bell-like blooms often open a pinkish-mauve colour and gradually turn brilliant white. The flowers stand out particularly well, because the main leaves do not appear until after the main blooming period.

An abundance of this wildflower is a very good indicator that a wood is of great age, because this member of the buttercup family (Ranunculaceae) takes a long time to become fully established.

Bluebell *(Hyacinthoides non-scripta)*

In spring many woods and shady roadside verges are carpeted with bluebells, and on calm evenings the air there is filled with the fragrance of these delicate wild hyacinths.

< 15mm >

In parts of Wales you may see 'bluebells' with white, pink or mauve flowers. Some of these are probably garden escapes of the Spanish bluebell, which occurs in all of those colours, but as often nowadays they may be hybrid crosses between our native bluebell and the introduced species.

Children have always loved gathering bunches of bluebells to take home, although they last no time at all as cut flowers. Because bluebells reproduce mainly via their bulbs, picking the flowers might not do much harm; however, if its leaves are damaged a bluebell plant may die.

Daffodil *(Narcissus pseudonarcissus)*

In spring, hedgerows and woodland edges throughout Wales are lined with daffodils, the St David's Day emblem of the principality.

< 60mm >

The lovely little **Tenby daffodil**, *Narcissus obvallaris,* (left) is considered by many to be a native of southwest Wales; however that is far from certain. What *is* clear is that very few remain in the wild as a result of its popularity in the nineteenth century, when large numbers were dug up and transported for sale in England. A daffodil – possibly even the Tenby daffodil itself – is one of two plant emblems of Wales; the leek, of course, is the other.

Many cultivated daffodils have escaped into the wild, and you are likely to see a wide range of varieties in Wales, especially on roadsides and in hedgerows near to towns and villages.

Early-purple Orchid *(Orchis mascula)*

Early-purple orchids grow in hedgerows, beside footpaths and on broadleaf woodland edges that they share with bluebells and lesser celandines. The leaves of this common orchid - the first each year to appear in Wales - are usually, but not always, spotted.

At first early-purple orchids have a pleasant perfume perceived by some people as quite akin to that of lily of the valley, but as the flowers fade so the smell becomes less enjoyable.

This lovely orchid was once both abundant and widespread, but it has suffered badly from modern farming practices that have destroyed much of its natural habitat and the root fungi upon which it and other wild orchids depend.

In times past, among many local names these orchids were variously referred to as adder's meat, blue butchers, and goosey ganders.

< 15mm >

Although the flowers of the early-purple orchid are usually some shade of pink or purple, once in a while you may come across a specimen with brilliant white flowers.

Jan   Feb   Mar   Apr   May   Jun   Jul   Aug   Sep   Oct   Nov   Dec   *17*

Wood-sorrel *(Oxalis acetosella)*

<15mm>

Shady places beside streams are much favoured by this delicate spring flower, which is very tolerant of acid soils. At night, not only do wood-sorrel flowers close up but the leaves also fold together rather like a fan; they will also react in this way if you touch them.

The trefoil leaves of wood-sorrel distinguish it from the more abundant wood anemone.

In well-shaded places, the petals of this delicate flower retain deep pink-purple veins.

Once the flowers have died, wood-sorrel plants can be mistaken for clover, because the leaves are so similar.

Columbine *(Aquilegia vulgaris)*

< 40mm >

Also known as granny bonnets, columbine is a member of the buttercup family, Ranunculaceae. This wildflower of late spring and early summer loves damp shady banks.

The individual flowers have five tubular petals and short, hooked spurs. Native to Northern Ireland, it is likely that the flowers now seen in the wild in most other parts of Britain, including Wales, are the result of garden escapes.

Truly wild columbine flowers are blue or purple, but colonies of many other colours are now naturalised throughout Wales. It is a poisonous plant and has long had dark connotations: posies of columbine flowers were presented as a message of condemnation to women who were considered to be cuckolds.

Columbine can grow up to a metre tall, and despite its slender structure the stems cope remarkably well in high winds and heavy rain.

Jan Feb Mar Apr May Jun Jul Aug Sep Oct Nov Dec *19*

Coltsfoot *(Tussilago farfara)*

40m

As soon as we get the first warm days of spring, coltsfoot blooms. These dandelion-like flowers are plentiful in Wales and particularly common on disturbed soil beside roads.

< 40mm >

The flower stems are reddish at first, turning to green as the flowers mature.

In the pictures above and left, the large rounded leaves are hardly visible; like those of butterbur, they grow rapidly once the flowers have seeded.

Jan Feb Mar Apr May Jun Jul Aug Sep Oct Nov Dec

Ramsons *(Allium ursinum)*

< 40mm >

A plant that carpets woodland floors and roadsides in damp places throughout Wales, ramsons – also known as wild garlic - advertises its presence by its strong smell.

The name ramsons is thought to come from the Anglo Saxon word 'hramsa', meaning rank. (Milk from cows that have eaten ramsons is said to taste rank or bitter.)

All parts of this plant, which is a close relative of the leek, are edible. The bulb itself tastes rather milder than a garlic clove.

Jan   Feb   Mar   Apr   May   Jun   Jul   Aug   Sep   Oct   Nov   Dec   *21*

Dog Violet *(Viola riviniana)*

< **20mm** >

Few wildflowers can be as well known as the violet, but because of its habit of hiding among other vegetation beneath hedgerows this spring flower is not always easy to spot. Dog violets, which are not scented, spread by means of runners.

Sweet violets, *Viola odorata* (left), which occur in the woods, do have a scent. The flowers are often white, but they also occur in various shades of pink or blue.

Whereas the dog violet is almost hairless, sweet violets have lightly downy stems and leaves.

Lords and Ladies *(Arum maculatum)*

These strange spring flowers first become apparent in January, when tall green spikes emerge from the ground. Inside each spike is a thick flower stem bearing a pale cream compound flower (the male part being immediately above the female).

The flower spike opens into a cowl-like hood and then gradually changes colour from pale green to purple before the hood decays, leaving a stem on which bright red berries (inset in the picture above) develop and ripen in the autumn.

Another common name given to this poisonous plant, which is frequently to be seen beside woodland paths and shady lanes in Wales, is cuckoopint – undoubtedly because the first flowers appear just as the cuckoos arrive in April.

Just one more of the numerous names that this fascinating wildflower has attracted is the wonderfully descriptive title of 'parson-in-the-pulpit'.

< 80mm >

Three-cornered Leek *(Allium triquetrum)*

Green veins on the white petals of this lovely bell-shaped flower immediately distinguish it from white wild hyacinths (white 'bluebells') that bloom at the same time of year.

< 15mm >

Now widely naturalized in Wales, especially in mild coastal areas, this alien species was imported from the western Mediterranean and has been planted in gardens in Britain since the mid 1700s. In parts of southern Wales this plant has spread rapidly, blanketing and killing the native wildflowers; its eradication is both time-consuming and back-breaking.

Three-cornered leek thrives in damp, partially shaded areas such as woodland edges and the banks of ditches on the northern side of hedgerows. The flowers are pollinated by insects, and the ripe seeds have been known to be dispersed by ants.

Bugle *(Ajuga reptans)*

50mm

A member of the mint family, this low creeping perennial is a common sight in woodland edges, footpaths and churchyards. Bugle propagates mainly by throwing rooting runners.

The first flowers appear in April, and blooming continues until late June or early July. Where this plant creates large patches it is a great attraction for butterflies.

The bronze tint to the upper leaves is a characteristic that helps separate bugle from the many otherwise similar members of the mint family.

A related species, the **pyramidal bugle** (*Ajuga pyramidalis*) is in decline nationally and is now very scarce; it has not been recorded in Wales in recent years.

Yellow Archangel *(Lamiastrum galeobdolon)*

Another member of the mint family, this perennial spring flower is sometimes referred to as yellow deadnettle. It is most commonly found in damp places with partial shade.

< 15mm >

A possible explanation for the heavenly name of this plant is that, despite the similarity of its leaves to those of stinging nettles, it is entirely angelic in behaviour and does not sting.

Greater Stitchwort *(Stellaria holostea)*

20mm

Greater stitchwort is a straggly perennial that does not appreciate waterlogged situations, and so in some of the wettest parts of North Wales it is mainly confined to slopes. Elsewhere this is one of the most abundant of wayside spring wildflowers.

The flowers of **lesser stitchwort**, *Stellaria graminea*, (left) are little more than half the size of those of greater stitchwort and the petals more deeply divided; they appear from May to August.

This acid-loving plant also favours grassy banks. Like its larger and more widespread cousin, it is a member of the pink family, Caryophyllaceae.

Butcher's Broom *(Ruscus aculeatus)*

< 10mm >

Instead of leaves this strange woodland plant has leaf-shaped flattened stems, called cladodes, typically 3cm long. In late winter, tiny green flowers (see below) appear in the centre of some of the cladodes, and there in summer red berries develop.

< 5mm >

This plant's common name refers to its use by butchers for scrubbing clean their wooden chopping blocks. Also known as knee holly, this prickly member of the lily family rarely grows to more than a metre in height.

The sap of butcher's broom is a mild diuretic and has many uses in herbal medicine.

Garlic Mustard *(Alliaria petiolata)*

Leaves of garlic mustard have been used for centuries to flavour sauces for serving with fish or lamb; they can also be used in spring salads. The plant resembles a stinging nettle, but it is easily distinguished by its white flowers and, later, by the long seedpods.

< 10mm >

Garlic mustard is also known as Jack-by-the-hedge, because it so often grows beneath hedgerows.

As with other members of the cabbage family (Brassicaceae) the leaves of this wildflower are a major food source for caterpillars of the orange-tip butterfly, inset left. (Only the males actually have orange-tipped wings!)

Jan Feb Mar Apr May Jun Jul Aug Sep Oct Nov Dec *29*

Red Campion *(Silene dioica)*

< **20mm** >

This splendidly showy plant of hedgerows and woodland margins is much loved for its dense flower masses that last all through the summer and into autumn.

Banks beneath roadside hedgerows throughout Wales often sport a rich mixture of red campion, greater stitchwort, bluebells and many other spring flowers. Many Pembrokeshire lanes, such as the one shown here, are particularly colourful in May, before cow parsley, bracken and other tall summer vegetation take over.

Male and female flowers are borne on separate plants, and because red campion readily hybridises with the closely related white campion (*Silene latifolia*) you may see banks swathed with flowers ranging from very pale pink to a lovely deep magenta-red.

Jan   Feb   Mar   Apr   May   Jun   Jul   Aug   Sep   Oct   Nov   Dec

White Campion *(Silene latifolia)*

< 30mm >

A wildflower of waysides and disturbed ground, white campion is more common on the eastern side of Wales than the west; its flowers are larger than those of red campion.

< 20mm >

Two other campions found in Wales could be mistakenly recorded as white campion:

Bladder campion, *Silene vulgaris* (left), has a shorter flowering season than the other campion species, blooming from May to August. It is found most frequently on disturbed ground such as motorway embankments. In Wales this attractive wildflower is most common in the south and the east.

Sea campion (*Silene uniflora*) is mainly confined to coastal cliffs; it has flowers similar to but somewhat larger than those of bladder campion.

Bee Orchid *(Ophrys apifera)*

40mm

The bee orchid, named for the appearance of its flowers, thrives in limestone areas.

Conspicuous and spectacular, bee orchids can grow to a height of 40 cm. They are often to be seen on motorway verges and roundabouts where limestone chippings have been used in the construction of roads or drainage channels.

Male bees, attracted by the appearance and by 'false pheromones' that these orchids emit, may alight on the flowers; there are, however, no confirmed reports of pollination success by this method. Whatever the case, it is certainly true that bee orchids are also able to reproduce by self-pollination.

In common with many other orchids, the bee orchid can appear almost magically in large numbers on disturbed ground and then disappear completely for many years.

Jan   Feb   Mar   Apr   May   Jun   Jul   Aug   Sep   Oct   Nov   Dec

Rosebay Willowherb *(Chamerion angusifolium)*

This tall flower, also referred to as fireweed because it colonises burnt ground, is equally at home on woodland edges and roadside banks, where it often grows in large clumps.

80mm

Rosebay willowherb was introduced from North America in the 18th century as a garden plant, but because of its invasive behaviour it quickly became naturalized throughout Britain and is now very common in all parts of Wales. Its flowers are a valuable source of nectar for bees during the day and for moths at night.

There is a hint of sadness associated with the appearance of these flowers, because they herald the onset of autumn and the imminent disappearance of most of the floral colour from our countryside.

Many other members of the willowherb family occur in Wales, including **great willowherb** (*Epilobium hirsutum*), another large variety that is often found on riverbanks, and **marsh willowherb** (*Epilobium palustre*), a paler and much more delicate little flower.

Evening Primrose *(Oenothera biennis)*

40mm

You will see plenty of these splendid summer flowers on waste ground, beside railway tracks, and occasionally even on sand dunes. They cope very well with dry conditions.

Introduced in the 17th century from North America, where there are some 50 species of evening primroses, this upright biennial is now a very common sight throughout Wales. The flowers do indeed open in the evening, when they are pollinated by moths.

Much used as a herbal medicine, evening primrose oil (oil extracted from the seeds) has been granted UK pharmaceutical licences for the treatment of certain kinds of eczema as well as mastalgia (breast pain).

Across Wales you may see other species of evening primroses, most of which are occasional garden escapes, and they tend to hybridise with the common evening primrose making specific identification very difficult.

Honeysuckle *(Lonicera periclymenum)*

This sweet-scented climber graces summer hedgerows with its alluring flowers. It is most strongly perfumed in the evening, at which time it attracts swirling swarms of moths which, as they gather nectar, pollinate the flowers.

Honeysuckle, once commonly called woodbine, has a long blooming period, and so it is quite common to see the red fruit berries (inset, above) alongside honeysuckle blossom in autumn. This exotic looking wildflower is a clockwise climber and can rapidly cover trees up to six metres tall.

80mm

Shining Cranesbill *(Geranium lucidum)*

>9mm<

One of the first wild geraniums to appear in the hedgerows of Wales, shining cranesbill gets its name from its glossy, wax-like leaves. The tiny pink flowers are borne sparsely.

>15mm<

Cranesbills are so called because of the long pointed 'beak' that appears at the top of each fruit pod.

Herb Robert, *Geranium robertianum* (left), another member of the geranium family, Geraniaceae, is also very common in Welsh hedgerows and dry stone walls.

Wherever wild geranium plants get very little moisture, their leaves turn a startling bright red as the summer draws on.

Silverweed *(Potentilla anserina)*

< 20mm >

This creeping member of the rose family, Rosaceae, spreads by means of runners that root at leaf nodes. Early in the year its leaves are silver on both upper and lower surfaces, and the undersides of the leaves often remain silver right through to autumn.

>20mm<

Silverweed loves damp places, and it is often to be found on well-trodden footpaths through permanent pasture or beside shady country lanes.

Another member of the rose family with five petals, **creeping cinquefoil**, *Potentilla reptans* (left), can be distinguished from silverweed by its leaves, each of which comprises five long, serrated fingers.

Jan   Feb   Mar   Apr   May   Jun   Jul   Aug   Sep   Oct   Nov   Dec   *37*

Ground ivy *(Glechoma hederacea)*

>10mm<

Ground ivy, a member of the mint family, is commonly found in woodlands and on waysides in Wales, often along with betony and other members of the Lamiaceae.

Ground ivy flowers are blue or mauve, and they are nothing like as densely packed around the stem as those of most other wildflowers from the same family.

These shy little wildflowers are common along hedgerows and woodland edges in Wales.

Considered to have been fairly widespread across southern England and Wales, **meadow clary** *(Salvia pratensis)*, with its striking blue flowers, is now close to becoming extinct in Britain. Surviving in only just 20 sites, including one in southeast Wales, this lime-loving member of the mint family has been adversely affected by changes in land use. Ironically, attempts at its reintroduction have met with little success even though other impacts of mankind seem to be making the climate in Wales rather more hospitable to this and several other 'lost' species that are still to be seen in other European countries.

Welsh Poppy *(Meconopsis cambrica)*

< 35mm >

Unusual elsewhere in Britain save as a garden escape, this lovely poppy thrives in Wales.

Welsh poppies enjoy cool weather and need constant moisture; they therefore tend to favour shady locations.

Through the summer months, many a wooded lane or rocky gulley in Snowdonia or mid Wales is brightened by the bobbing yellow heads of these delicate wildflowers.

Garden varieties derived from the Welsh poppy include flowers with orange petals as well as 'double' poppies.

Jan   Feb   Mar   Apr   May   Jun   Jul   Aug   Sep   Oct   Nov   Dec   *39*

Foxglove *(Digitalis purpurea)*

Whenever woodland or wayside slopes are disturbed – for example when timber is harvested - foxgloves are likely to appear in great profusion in the following year.

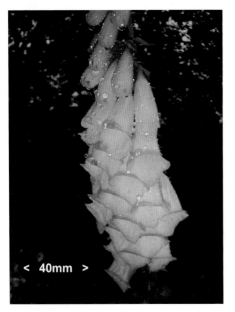

< 40mm >

Such stately biennials, foxgloves nevertheless bring with them a kind of sadness, because they signal the end of spring, with all its freshness, and the onset of high summer.

Foxgloves can grow to two metres in height and have up to eighty bell-like flowers in long spikes. Although they are usually pink-purple, very occasionally in Wales you will come across wild foxgloves with white flowers.

Despite their beauty and innocuous common name, foxgloves are in fact poisonous plants. They have been given many other names including fairy bells and fairy gloves Young children find the finger-sized bells quite irresistible and use them as glove puppets.

Dog Rose *(Rosa canina)*

Although dog roses can be self supporting, the tallest specimens rely on other plants for support. They provide wonderful summer displays in hedgerows throughout Wales.

During the winter months the seed pods, called hips, adorn hedges… that is until hungry birds find them.

There are several other species of wild rose, including the white field rose and the burnet rose. Brambles, raspberries and cloudberries are also relatives, as too are wild strawberries.

Teasel *(Dipsacus fullonum)*

50mm

The teasel is a close relative of the various species of scabious. This stately plant is particularly common on motorway cuttings and beside railway tracks as well as on woodland edges and gravelly or lightly shale-strewn wasteland.

The pale purple flower heads of teasel are at their finest in summer, but many people like to pick them and keep them as dried flowers for indoor decoration. As with all wild flowers, taking too many from one place can only mean fewer flowers in future years – so why not settle for taking photographs?

During the 'carding' process, dried teasel heads were used to tease out the fibres of wool and so create a tangle-free roll ready for spinning - hence the common name teasel.

At the National Woollen Museum of Wales, near Newcastle Emlyn, carding pads complete with teasel heads can still be seen; they look rather like shortened cricket bats covered in Velcro. Although initially the craftsmen (called fullers) who carded wool used our native wild teasel, an imported species, *Dipsacus sativus*, with hooked spines proved more effective and it soon secured the common name of fuller's teasel.

Left: Teasel seed heads remain standing throughout the winter months.

Scarlet Pimpernel *(Anagallis arvensis)*

A low-growing annual blooming from May through to October, scarlet pimpernel is far from elusive: it springs up on disturbed wasteland and, as seen above, through car-park shale.

< 10mm >

A member of the primrose family, Primulaceae, and a 'lark' among wildflowers, in Wales the flowers of scarlet pimpernel open around 8am, and they close soon after 2pm even on sunny days. As one of its alternative names, poor-man's weatherglass, suggests, the flowers also remain stubbornly closed during very dull or damp weather.

Unusually, rather than dropping individually the petals of scarlet pimpernel remain as an intact ring that falls to the ground like a discarded miniskirt.

Occasionally you may come across blue variants (left) of this neat little wildflower.

Wall Pennywort *(Umbilicus rupestris)*

< 30mm >

A member of the stonecrop family, wall pennywort has leaves in the form of a shallow goblet. It is commonly found growing on walls and rocky banks in lightly-shaded areas.

This succulent plant is also known as navelwort – a reference to the umbilical leaf shape (below).

Sometimes the pallid spikes of bell-shaped flowers of wall pennywort turn pale pink as the fruits ripen, and in the driest locations the whole of the plant usually takes on a deep pink hue.

It the past several medicinal properties were ascribed to this plant, and hence the term 'wort' was appended to its common name. The juice was taken as a treatment for epilepsy and for inflammation of the liver, while the leaves were used to treat piles, gout and chilblains.

Comfrey *(Symphytum species)*

< 40mm >

The bell-shaped flowers of common comfrey (*Symphytum officinale*) are usually cream or dull purple, but throughout Wales there are also many hybrid forms with pink, mauve or blue flowers. Comfrey thrives in damp hedgerows and woodland edges.

Russian comfrey (*Symphytum x uplandicum*) has now become the most common kind of comfrey in Wales, and it is particularly abundant in parts of the Wye and Monnow valleys.

In medieval times, comfrey delighted in the name of 'bone-set' – indeed in certain countries its leaves are still used today as poultice dressings for bruises.

Concerns have been expressed about the safety of using this plant in herbal medicines. Although some herbalists currently recommend taking comfrey extracts to soothe inflamed mucous membranes, in the 1980s scientists reported that certain kinds of comfrey contain chemicals known as pyrrolizidine alkaloids that can cause serious liver damage.

Field Bindweed *(Convolvulus arvensis)*

< 20mm >

Despite its common name, in Wales this species of bindweed is most often seen on roadside verges and wasteland. It has pink or sometimes white flared bell-shaped flowers.

< 40mm >

The various species of bindweeds can be difficult to eradicate from gardens. The roots travel great distances and are extremely brittle; even the tiniest piece of root left in the ground can produce a new plant within weeks.

Hedge bindweed, *Calystegia sepium* (left) is a similar climber with larger flowers that can be either white or pink.

Jan   Feb   Mar   Apr   May   Jun   Jul   Aug   Sep   Oct   Nov   Dec

Betony *(Stachys officinalis)*

< **30mm** >

Betony, a member of the mint family, Lamiaceae, occurs most frequently in hedgerows and at woodland edges. The flower heads, borne on almost leafless stems, occasionally grow to a height of 40cm, although 25cm is more typical.

Various medicinal powers have been ascribed to betony. The Romans used it to treat headaches, liver disease and bronchial complaints, and in the Middle Ages people wore it in their hats to deter witches and to ward off evil spirits. (In Shropshire, betony was once commonly referred to as 'the devil's plaything'.)

More innocently, perhaps, betony has also been used in dyeing.

Jan   Feb   Mar   Apr   May   Jun   Jul   Aug   Sep   Oct   Nov   Dec   *47*

Broadleaved Helleborine *(Epipactis helleborine)*

< 40mm >

Helleborines are members of the orchid family, and like many other orchids this species is relatively uncommon in Wales. Broad-leaved helleborines favour woodland glades.

This large-flowered orchid grows to a height of 25cm to 80cm. The flowers, which are aligned on one side of the stem, vary in colour from a greenish-yellow through mauve to a reddish-purple.

Of the nearly 50 species of orchids in Britain, this one is still relatively common. The marsh helleborine *(Epipactis palustris)* is common in the dune slacks of Wales, while other helleborines are relatively scarce and the magnificent dark-red helleborine *(Epipactis atrorubens)* is now limited to just two sites.

Ox-eye Daisy *(Leucanthemum vulgare)*

60mm

The ox-eye daisy, also referred to as dog daisy, marguerite and moon penny, is often seen in great profusion on roadsides and on dry slopes beside woodlands in Wales.

In sheltered places, ox-eye daisies can reach a height of 80cm, whereas on wind-swept slopes they adapt to the adverse conditions by crouching low among the grasses.

This wildflower seems frequently to have been linked with St. Mary Magdalen - hence the name maudlin-wort, by which it was known to the great herbalist Gerard.

Jan   Feb   Mar   Apr   May   Jun   Jul   Aug   Sep   Oct   Nov   Dec   *49*

Green Alkanet *(Pentaglottis sempervirens)*

This tall plant of woodland edges and shady hedgerows is locally plentiful in limestone areas of Denbighshire and Pembrokeshire, but it is seldom seen in some parts of Wales.

< 15mm >

The name alkanet comes from an Arabic word meaning henna - and a red dye can indeed be obtained from the roots of this plant.

Flowers of green alkanet are similar to those of the various forget-me-nots, which is perhaps not so surprising because they are all members of the Borage family (Boraginaceae).

Fox and Cubs *(Pilosella aurantiaca)*

20mm

An attractive member of the daisy family, Asteraceae (Compositae), often grown in gardens as well as occurring in the wild, this hawkweed prefers well-drained soil. You may see vast numbers on a roadside slope one year and then none at all the following year.

This complex group of wildflowers also includes the many species of hawkbits and hawksbeards, all of which have dandelion-like flowers and, like those pictured on the left, are commonly found on wasteland and beside well-trodden footpaths on light soils. Precise identification of many of these species is very difficult, but careful study of the leaves is often a help.

It has been alleged that hawks eat these kinds of flowers and that doing so improves their ability to spot prey from a great height; indeed, there are even reports of people having eaten the flowers of fox and cubs in the belief that this would somehow improve their eyesight.

White Deadnettle *(Lamium album)*

50mm

Much more nettle-like in appearance than is its relative the red deadnettle (see below), this member of the mint family is commonly found on roadsides and beside hedgerows.

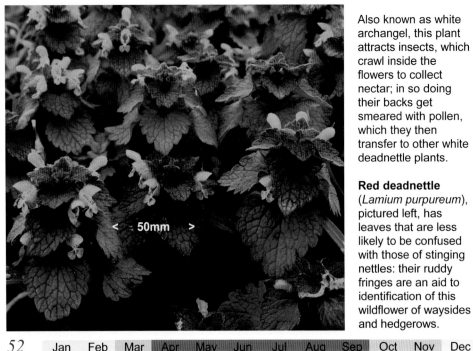

50mm

Also known as white archangel, this plant attracts insects, which crawl inside the flowers to collect nectar; in so doing their backs get smeared with pollen, which they then transfer to other white deadnettle plants.

Red deadnettle (*Lamium purpureum*), pictured left, has leaves that are less likely to be confused with those of stinging nettles: their ruddy fringes are an aid to identification of this wildflower of waysides and hedgerows.

Common Spotted-orchid *(Dactylorhiza fuchsii)*

Wherever the soil is not too acidic, the common spotted-orchid is among the most frequently found of orchid species in Wales. It thrives in unimproved grassland, scrub, open woodland and even on some motorway verges.

A large colony of common spotted-orchids, along with the southern marsh-orchid (*Dactylorhiza praetermissa*), can be seen at Aberthaw Power Station, near Barry.

Ranging in colour from deep pink through mauve to almost white, these orchids also vary in size from a mere 10cm to over 60cm tall.

< **40mm** >

Stinking Hellebore *(Helleborus foetidus)*

< 25mm >

Despite its unfortunate name, stinking hellebore is a striking and very beautiful flower. It is yet another member of the buttercup family, Ranunculaceae.

The plants can grow to 80cm in height and they have bright green-yellow flowers with distinctive purple edges; the flowers occur in clusters.

Stinking hellebore, which has distinctive dark-green palmate leaves, can be found in damp, well-shaded places such as under roadside hedges and at the edge of deciduous woods.

54   Jan   Feb   Mar   Apr   May   Jun   Jul   Aug   Sep   Oct   Nov   Dec

Borage *(Borago officinalis)*

< **30mm** >

A beautiful introduced wildflower, borage has a juice that tastes and smells rather like cucumber; not surprisingly, therefore, it has acquired many culinary and herbal uses.

This annual plant, growing to typically 60cm tall, seems to prefer disturbed ground. It is a native of southern Europe and now a very common wayside plant throughout most of Europe, including some parts of Wales.

The Romans may have been responsible for introducing borage to Britain; however, in many places it now grows in the wild simply because it has escaped from gardens, becoming established on waste ground and road verges.

Borage is grown commercially for the oil that its seeds contain. The leaves can be used in salads or in other dishes in place of spinach, and the flower petals make an edible ornamental addition to drinks as well as to salads.

Jan   Feb   Mar   Apr   May   Jun   Jul   Aug   Sep   Oct   Nov   Dec   *55*

Wild Strawberry *(Fragaria vesca)*

< 10mm >

The strawberry is a member of the rose family (Rosaceae), and wild strawberries are very common in Wales. Because of their low-growing habit and the small size of their flowers and fruits, it is not always easy to spot them below hedgerows and on grassy banks.

Wild strawberries bloom mainly in spring and early summer, although this is one wildflower that can invariably be found blooming somewhere in Wales during every month of the year.

From July onwards, the fruits ripen and provide the essential ingredients for tastier desserts than can be produced from most cultivated varieties of strawberries.

Barren Strawberry *(Potentilla sterilis)* occurs in similar wayside habitats but is easily distinguished from the fruit-bearing wild strawberry because it has flowers (left) with distinct gaps between the petals.

Biting Stonecrop *(Sedum acre)*

Biting stonecrop has bitter-tasting leaves, for which it was awarded its Latin name 'acre', meaning sharp. This low-growing member of the stonecrop family is an evergreen.

< 15mm >

Also known as wall pepper, biting stonecrop is found in dry, rocky places such as old stone walls and disused railway tracks as well as, occasionally, on sand dunes.

Jan Feb Mar Apr May Jun Jul Aug Sep Oct Nov Dec *57*

White Bryony *(Bryonia dioica)*

15mm

A wildflower of hedgerows and field margins in chalky areas, white bryony belongs to the gourd family. Female (above) and male flowers differ slightly and grow on separate plants.

In the past white bryony was used as a purgative; it has even been known to kill young children who have eaten its attractive red berries.

Black bryony (*Tamus communis*), a member of the yam family, is a hedgerow climber with rather undistinguished greenish-yellow flowers typically 4mm to 6mm across. In autumn the bright red berries of black bryony (left) make brilliant displays long after the leaves and main stems have shriveled and died back.

Jan   Feb   Mar   Apr   May   Jun   Jul   Aug   Sep   Oct   Nov   Dec

Great Mullein *(Verbascum thapsus)*

< 25mm >

The largest of several wild mulleins found in the British Isles, great mullein is a most imposing wildflower and often occurs in large groups. Another of its common names is Aaron's rod.

Growing to a height of two metres, this conspicuous plant has furry grey or sometimes almost white leaves that cling tightly to the stem. The flowers open more or less at random, so that it is rare to see a mullein with the whole raceme blooming; more often there will be a few flowers open near the tip and one or two much lower down, with the middle section in bloom only after the petals have fallen from the earlier opening flowers.

Great mullein stalks often persist into the following summer; indeed, the ancient Greeks and Romans are recorded as having coated them in tallow and used them as funeral torches.

Throughout most of Wales this is the only kind of mullein to be seen in any numbers.

Coping well with dry conditions, this instantly recognizable wildflower sometimes lines tracks on slopes where the soil is thin and limey. Less commonly, it grows in mildly acidic soil, and so while most abundant in eastern Wales occasional specimens can be found throughout the country.

Mulleins are members of the figwort family, Scrophulariaceae.

Birdsfoot Trefoil *(Lotus corniculatus)*

< 15mm >

Also known as bacon and eggs, this low-growing member of the pea family adds a splash of colour to roadside verges and dry grassy paths. The flowers may be all yellow or yellow tinged with orange or red – or occasionally entirely orange.

< 40mm >

Greater birdsfoot trefoil (*Lotus pedunculatus*) is a plant of damp and shady roadside verges and woodland rides; it also occurs in marshes. This is much more of a scrambling climber than its low-growing 'lesser' cousin. Although lacking the tendrils that most climbing members of the pea family use to cling on to other plants, greater birdsfoot trefoil can grow up to a metre tall. Its flowers, which appear at the same time as those of lesser birdsfoot trefoil, are always deep yellow.

Meadow Vetchling *(Lathyrus pratensis),* shown on the left, is another very similar member of the pea family, distinguished by dark lines on the clear yellow (rather than yellow-orange) background .

Harebells *(Campanula rotundifolia)*

< 25mm >

Most common on roadsides on higher ground in Wales, this delicate summer flower grows in great abundance on banks, sparse hedgerows and well drained woodland edges.

The origin of the name harebell is far from clear. Witches were said to use these flowers in spells that enabled them to turn themselves into hares; alternatively, the name may simply be a reference to the fact that harebells are most commonly found in the kinds of places frequented by hares.

In Scotland these bell-shaped little flowers are also referred to as *'the bluebells of Scotland'*, and so there is the possibility of their confusion with the earlier-blooming bluebells of the lily family. Harebells are not lilies but rather members of the bellflower family, Campanulaceae.

Jan   Feb   Mar   Apr   May   Jun   Jul   Aug   Sep   Oct   Nov   Dec   *61*

Sheepsbit *(Jasione montana)*

< 20mm >

A low-growing wayside biennial plant of dry places, sheepsbit is particularly common in Wales on banks beneath sparse hedgerows, where it copes well with strong winds. Despite its daisy-like appearance, this very variable wildflower is a member of the bellflower family, Campanulaceae.

< 25mm >

Sheepsbit is often confused with **devilsbit scabious**, *Succisa pratensis*, or occasionally with dark specimens of **field scabious**, *Knautia arvensis* (left). These two latter species, both members of the teasel family, can also be seen in dry, grassy places in Wales.

In Wales, sheepsbit is generally more common and widespread than either of its more mauve look-alikes.

Ivy-leaved Toadflax *(Cymbalaria muralis)*

A creeping plant mainly found growing in walls, ivy-leaved toadflax thrives in sunny positions where its roots can get a grip in sparse, quick-draining soil.

< 12mm >

This long-flowering member of the figwort family (the Scrophulariaceae) is so widespread across Wales that it is hard to believe it is a garden escape. Ivy-leaved toadflax was originally imported to Britain from Italy in 1630 among a consignment of marble and other building stone.

Jan   Feb   Mar   Apr   May   Jun   Jul   Aug   Sep   Oct   Nov   Dec   63

Common Toadflax *(Linaria vulgaris)*

< 20mm >

At its best long after most spring flowers have finished blooming, this perennial colonises waste land but is also seen on roadside verges and well drained grassy hedge banks.

< 10mm >

Pale toadflax, *Linaria repens* (left), has grey-streaked flowers and can be seen blooming on disused railway tracks and dry grassy banks throughout Wales.

Bees love these flowers, but they have some difficulty extracting nectar from the long spurs. As toadflax flowers mature, the orange patch on the mouth usually becomes more noticeable. The toadflaxes cope well with drought conditions

Some people mistakenly identify toadflaxes as 'snapdragons'; the spurs behind the flower heads of all toadflaxes are a helpful distinguishing feature.

Woody Nightshade *(Solanum dulcamara)*

< 15mm >

Woody nightshade is also known as bittersweet. All parts of the plant are poisonous, and children have been known to die from eating the attractive red berries (inset, above).

< 30mm >

Deadly nightshade, *Atropa belladonna* (left), is now a rare plant in Britain and occurs only in chalk and limestone rich areas. In Wales it is confined to the Marches and the Severn Valley. The rather drab purple flowers of deadly nightshade are bell-shaped; they eventually produce round berries up to 2cm in diameter that start off green and gradually turn black and glossy (inset, left).

As its common name implies, this plant is extremely poisonous.

Both woody nightshhade and deadly nightshade are members the family Solanaceae (as also are tomatoes and potatoes).

Woodland Wildflowers in Wales

The habitats provided by woodland edges and clearings, roadside verges and hedgerows, footpaths and bridleways are tremendously varied. As a result they are home to a great diversity of wildflowers, some favouring shade and damp, others thriving in the windswept and sun-scorched conditions of quick-draining slopes.

Wales has such a wealth of accessible woodland and scrubland, much of it cared for by dedicated conservationists on either a professional or a voluntary basis. Indeed, many of the National Trust (www.nationaltrust.org.uk) sites in Wales, such as Colby Woodland Gardens, in Pembrokeshire, are popular venues for wildflower enthusiasts.

The Woodland Trust (www.woodlandtrust.org.uk) looks after more than a thousand woods or groups of woods of which at least a hundred are within Wales. Other Welsh woodlands are managed in partnership by the Forestry Commission (www.forestry.gov.uk) and the Countryside Council for Wales (www.ccw.gov.uk) not only for their timber but also to conserve their faunal and floral diversity. For example Newborough Forest, on the island of Anglesey, is home to no fewer than ten species of wild orchids including the bee orchid.

Flowers are vitally important to so many wild creatures, and so it is not surprising that the twelve major RSPB bird reserves in Wales (www.rspb.org.uk/wales) are also noted for the abundance and variety of wildflowers that they harbour. The National Parks of Pembrokeshire, Snowdonia and the Brecon Beacons (www.cnp.org.uk) also provide access to wonderful walks, many running beside or through woodland that is managed sympathetically for wildflowers, butterflies, birds and other wildlife.

The Wildlife Trust movement (www.wildlifetrust.org) is also very active in Wales, managing dozens of sites and reserves of which at least 50 per cent include scrub or woodland. For example, North Wales Wildlife Trust works with Plantlife (www.plantlife.org) and other partners to manage a reserve at Caeau Tan y Bwlch, on the Lleyn Peninsula, where visitors can see several orchid species and many other rare and lovely wildflowers.

A bonus of visiting sites and reserves managed by the organisations mentioned above is the chance to meet the rangers, wardens and conservation volunteers, who share so generously their wealth of knowledge. We have always been so inspired by their infectious passion for the Welsh countryside that they care for.